2192

Music Minus One Vocals

BIG BAND MALE STANDARDS
songs in the style of Frank Sinatra

Big Band Male Standards

songs in the style of Frank Sinatra

CONTENTS

ISBN 978-1-941566-89-3

MMO 2192

Serenade In Blue

Lyrics by Mack Gordon
Music by Harry Warren

I'll Never Smile Again

Words and Music by Ruth Lowe

A C#m7

I'll Nev -er Smile A - gain,

F#7 · Bmaj7 · C#m7 · D#m7 · Ddim7

un - til I smile at you. _____ I'll nev - er

C#m7 · F#7 · B

laugh a - gain. _____ What good would it do? _____ I'll

B G7#5 · F#7 · B

For tears would fill my eyes, my

C#m7(♭5) · G♭7#5 · Bmaj7 · A#9 · D# · A#7

heart would re - a - lize, that our ro - mance _____

D# · Ddim7 · C#m7 · F#7 Bmaj7 D#m7 Ddim7

___ is through. _____ I'll nev - er

C C#m7 · F#7 · Bmaj7 · C#m7

love a - gain I'm so in love with you. _____

D#m7 · Ddim7 · C#m7 · F#7

___ I'll nev - er thrill a - gain _____ to some - bod - y

Learnin' The Blues

Words and Music by Dolores "Vicki" Silvers

(Love Is) The Tender Trap

Words by Sammy Cahn
Music by James Van Heusen

The Song Is You
from MUSIC IN THE AIR

Lyrics by Oscar Hammerstein II
Music by Jerome Kern

They Can't Take That Away From Me

from SHALL WE DANCE

Music and Lyrics by George Gershwin and Ira Gershwin

I'll Be Seeing You

from RIGHT THIS WAY

Written by Irving Kahal and Sammy Fain

All Or Nothing At All

Words by Jack Lawrence
Music by Arthur Altman

This Love Of Mine

Words and Music by Sol Parker,
Henry W. Sanicola and Frank Sinatra

Prisoner Of Love

By Leo Robin, Clarence Gaskill
and Russ Colombo

Other Great Vocals from Music Minus One

Professional Sound Tracks, Vol. 1 ....MMO 2121
In The Still Of The Night • The Very Thought Of You • As Time Goes By • Yours • My Foolish Heart • I'll Be Seeing You • Harbour Lights • Red Sails In The Sunset

Professional Sound Tracks, Vol. 2 ....MMO 2122
The More I See You • Stardust • Moonlight Becomes You • I'm Getting Sentimental Over You • A Lovely Way To Spend An Evening • Long Ago And Far Away • I Don't Want To Walk Without You • You Belong To My Heart

Professional Sound Tracks, Vol. 3 ....MMO 2123
Embraceable You • I Wish I Knew • I'll Walk Alone • You'll Never Know • They Say It's Wonderful • Born Again • So In Love • The Girl That I Marry

Professional Sound Tracks, Vol. 4 ....MMO 2124
They Say It's Wonderful • My Defenses Are Down • Why Do I Love You? • Make Believe • Old Man River • If Ever I Would Leave You • Don Quixote (Man of La Mancha) • Dulcinea (Man of La Mancha) • The Impossible Dream (Man of La Mancha)

Professional Sound Tracks, Vol. 5 ....MMO 2125
Some Enchanted Evening • This Nearly Was Mine • Oh, What a Beautiful Morning • Surrey With The Fringe On Top • People Will Say We're In Love /Oklahoma • Memory • I Won't Send Roses • (Where Do I Begin) Love Story • Send In The Clowns

Professional Sound Tracks, Vol. 6 ....MMO 2126
I Only Have Eyes For You • You Go To My Head • Autumn In New York • My Funny Valentine • Am I Blue • I Don't Know Why (I Just Do) • You Took Advantage Of Me • I Cover The Waterfront • Someone To Watch Over Me

Night Club Standards, Vol. 1 (Female) ....MMO 2131
The More I See You • It Had to Be You • The Shadow of Your Smile • Watch What Happens • The Good Life • Call Me Irresponsible • Street of Dreams • I Should Care

Night Club Standards, Vol. 2 (Female) ....MMO 2132
They Can't Take That Away From Me • Come Rain Or Come Shine • Nice 'N' Easy • That Old Black Magic • It's Only A Paper Moon • Summer Wind • The Very Thought Of You • My Baby Just Cares for Me

Night Club Standards, Vol. 3 (Female) ....MMO 2133
I've Got The World On A String • Saturday Night (Is The Loneliest Night Of The Week • It's De-Lovely • Something's Gotta Give • Where Or When • Witchcraft • I Thought About You • Without A Song

Night Club Standards, Vol. 4 (Female) ....MMO 2134
The Best Is Yet To Come • I Could Have Danced All Night • They All Laughed • Oh, Look At Me Now • If I Had You • I'm Old Fashioned • A Nightingale Sang In Berkeley Square • The Lady Is A Tramp

The Great Ladies Of Jazz, Vol. 1 ....MMO 2135
A Good Man Is Hard To Find • Guess Who's In Town • Rockin' Chair • A Hundred Years From Today • It Don't Mean A Thing • Lullaby Of The Leaves • Goody Goody • Guess Who I Saw Today • What Is This Thing Called Love? • Moments Like This

The Great Ladies Of Jazz, Vol. 2 ....MMO 2136
Take The 'A; Train • Million Dollar Secret • Day Dream • Cried For You • Maybe • Too Late Now • Peel Me A Grape • Blue Gardenia • Street of Dreams • All That Jazz

Music Minus One
50 Executive Boulevard · Elmsford, New York 10523-1325
914-592-1188 · e-mail: info@musicminusone.com
www.musicminusone.com

MMO 2192

ISBN 978-1-941566-89-3